The Original
Smith Wigglesworth
Devotional

The Original Smith Wigglesworth Devotional

Orlando, FL

Larry Keefauver
General Editor

THE ORIGINAL SMITH WIGGLESWORTH DEVOTIONAL
Published by Creation House
Strang Communications Company
600 Rinehart Road
Lake Mary, Florida 32746
Web site: http://www.creationhouse.com

Unless otherwise noted, all Scripture quotations are from
the King James Version of the Bible.

Library of Congress Cataloging-in-Publication Data
Wigglesworth, Smith, 1859–1947.
   The Original Smith Wigglesworth Devotional / Larry
         Keefauver, general editor.
   1. Devotional calendars.   2. Christian life—Pentecostal
                  authors.
               I. Keefauver, Larry.
            ISBN: 0-88419-482-5
BV4811.W5923 1997   242'.2—dc21   97-23286
          78901234 RPG 87654321

Contents

Contents

Introduction

WELCOME TO THIS ninety-day journey with Smith Wigglesworth, the humble, anointed servant of God who dramatically shaped the early Pentecostal and Holiness movements on the continent and in the States.

Called a "twentieth-century apostle," Wigglesworth became a legend as God used him in an evangelistic and healing ministry. Born in 1859 in Menston, Yorkshire, England, he was converted in a Wesleyan Methodist meeting at age eight and pursued a career in plumbing. He married Polly Featherstone, and he and Polly operated a little mission in Bradford, England.

In 1907, in Sunderland, the forty-seven-year-old Wigglesworth received the baptism of the Holy Spirit, which radically changed him and transformed his ministry into a worldwide phenomenon. Literally thousands were saved and untold scores were healed by God's power as Wigglesworth preached powerful messages throughout the world. He went home to the Lord he loved in 1947 at the age of eighty-seven.

This book brings to you some exquisite gems of revelation about faith, prayer and healing. Receive power and inspiration for your daily walk with the Lord as you read the words of Smith Wigglesworth.

—LARRY KEEFAUVER
GENERAL EDITOR

The Amen of Faith

Now faith is the substance of things hoped for, the evidence of things not seen.
—HEBREWS 11:1

I BELIEVE THERE IS only one way to all the treasures of God, and that is the way of faith.

You get to know God by an open door of grace. He has made a way. It is a beautiful way that all His saints can enter in and find rest. The way is the way of faith. There isn't any other way.

Beloved, I see all the plan of life where God comes in and vindicates His power by making His presence felt. It is not by crying, nor groaning. It is because we believe. And yet, we have nothing to say about it. Sometimes it takes God a long time to bring us through the groaning and crying before we can believe.

Jesus, through the power of Your Holy Spirit, I seek the gift of supernatural faith that I may see the things of God. Amen.

Day 2

Overcoming Faith

*And this is the victory that overcometh
the world, even our faith.*

—1 JOHN 5:4

CHRIST IS the root and source of our faith.
When He is in what we believe for, it will
come to pass. No wavering. This is the principle: He who believes is definite. A definite
faith brings a definite experience and a definite
utterance. As our prayers rest upon the simple
principle of faith, nothing shall be impossible
to us.

The root principle of all this divine overcoming faith in the human heart is Christ.
When you are grafted deeply into Him, you
may win millions of lives to the faith. Jesus is
the Way, the Truth, and the Life, the secret to
every hard problem in your heart.

Lord Jesus, grant me overcoming faith to claim the impossible. Amen.

Day 3

God Is Greater

*So then faith cometh by hearing, and
hearing by the word of God.*
—ROMANS 10:17

DON'T STUMBLE at the Word. Believe that
God is greater than you are, greater than
your heart, greater than your thoughts.

Only He can establish you in righteousness
even when your thoughts and your knowledge
are absolutely against it.

The Word of God is true. If you will understand the truth, you can always be on line to
gain strength, overcome the world, and make
everything subject to you.

*Lord Jesus, renew my mind according
to Thy Word. Give me a desire for the
kind of faith that will overcome my
world. Amen.*

Saved Through Faith

For by grace are ye saved through faith; and that not of yourselves: it is the gift of God.

—Ephesians 2:8

HUMAN FAITH works and then waits for the wages. That is not saving faith. Then there is the gift of faith. "For by grace are ye saved through faith; and that not of yourselves: it is the gift of God." Faith is that which God gave you to believe. "Whosoever believeth that Jesus is the Christ is born of God" (1 John 5:1).

We read in 1 Corinthians 12:9, "To another faith by the same Spirit." When my faith fails, then another faith lays hold of me. One time I thought I had the Holy Ghost. Now I know the Holy Ghost has got me.

There is a difference between our hanging onto God and God's lifting us up. There is a difference between my having a desire and

God's desire filling my soul. There is a difference between natural compassion and the compassion of Jesus that never fails. Human faith fails but the faith of Jesus never fails.

> *Jesus, thank You for lifting me up.*
> *Thank You for filling my soul with an*
> *awareness of Your great desire for me.*
> *I seek You for the faith that never fails.*
> *Amen.*

Two Kinds of Faith

> *Wherefore also we pray always for you,*
> *that our God would . . . fulfil all the good*
> *pleasure of his goodness, and the work of*
> *faith with power.*
> —2 THESSALONIANS 1:11

THERE ARE TWO kinds of faith that God wants us to see. There is a natural faith and there is a saving faith. All people are born with the natural faith. Natural faith has limitations. Saving faith is a supernatural gift of God.

There is the gift of faith. It is the faith of Jesus given to us as we press in and on with God. I want to put before you this difference between our faith and the faith of Jesus.

Most people have come to where they have said, "Lord, I can go no further. I have gone so far and I can go no further. I have used all the faith I have, and I just have to stop now and wait."

As I saw in God's presence the limitation of

my natural faith, there came another faith, a supernatural faith that could not be denied, a faith that took the promise of God, a faith that believed God's Word.

> *Holy Spirit, give me supernatural faith as I press in and on with God. As I confront the circumstances of my life daily, help me to exercise my faith with Your power. Amen.*

Day 6

The Trial of Faith

That the trial of your faith, . . . though it be tried with fire, might be found unto praise and honour and glory at the appearing of Jesus Christ.

—1 Peter 1:7

GOLD PERISHETH. Faith never perisheth. It is more precious than gold, though it be tried by fire.

Beloved, as you are tested in the fire, the Master is cleaning away all that cannot bring out His image, cleaning away all the dross from your life, all the evil, until He sees His face reflected in your life.

Lord, I rejoice in my trials and sufferings as You refine my faith so that my life may reflect You. Amen.

Day 7

Living Faith

Therefore if any man be in Christ, he is a new creature: old things are passed away; behold, all things are become new.
—2 CORINTHIANS 5:17

NOW THE HEART cries out for a living faith with a deep vision of God. The world cannot produce it. Living faith is a place where we seek the Word so that when we pray we know God hears. Living faith comes into the presence of God, asking Him and believing Him for the answer, while having no fear.

I used to have a tremendous temper, going white with passion. My whole nature was not what God wanted. God knew that I could never be of service unless I was sanctified. For example, I was difficult to please at the table. My wife was a good cook, but there was always something wrong. After God sanctified me, she testified in a meeting that from the time

God touched me, I was pleased with everything she cooked.

It is our human spirit that has to be controlled by the Holy Spirit.

This world is full of stimulation. It is by faith, into a place of grace that all may see us new. Behold! Behold! Behold! What is it? The Holy Ghost is arousing our attention. He has something special to say. Behold, if you will believe, you can be sons of God in likeness, character, spirit, and actions.

> *Lord Jesus, I desire to be changed in Thy Presence. Make of me a new creation in Thee. Amen.*

Day 8

Only Believe

As soon as Jesus heard the word that was spoken, he saith unto the ruler of the synagogue, Be not afraid, only believe.
— MARK 5:36

THE IMPORTANCE of that chorus is the word *only* right in the midst of the chorus. If I can get you to see that when you get rid of yourself, all human help and everything else, and only have God behind you, you have reached a place of great reinforcement and continual success.

If you help yourself, to the measure you help yourself, you will find there are limitations to the life and power of God in you.

The one grand plan God has for us is *only believe.*

Absolute rest. Perfect submission. God has taken charge of the situation. You are absolutely brought into everything God has, because you dare only believe what He says.

God would have me press into your heart a living truth—only believe!

Only believe, only believe.
All things are possible,
Only believe.
Only believe, only believe.
All things are possible,
Only believe.

Jesus, what You have said, I believe.
Amen.

Day 9

Faith Is an Act

In the beginning was the Word, and the Word was with God, and the Word was God.

—JOHN 1:1

WE ARE SAVED by faith and kept by faith. Faith is a substance. It is also an evidence. God is. He is!

Faith goes on to act. It's a reality, a deposit of God, an almighty flame moving you to act, so that signs and wonders are manifest.

Faith takes you to the place where God reigns, where you are imbibing God's bountiful store. Unbelief is sin.

Jesus, You have created all that is. I desire to act on Your Word and to live by the power of Your Word. Amen.

Day 10

The Author of Our Faith

*Looking unto Jesus the author and fin-
isher of our faith*

—HEBREWS 12:2

HE IS THE AUTHOR of faith. Jesus became
the author of faith. God worked this
plan through Him by forming the worlds, by
making everything that there was by the word
of His power. Jesus was the Word; Christ.
God's divine principle is that God hath chosen
Jesus, ordained Him, clothed Him, and made
Him greater than all because of the joy given
by the love of God. Because of this exceeding,
abundant joy of saving the whole world, He
became the author of a living faith.

*Jesus, author of all faith, write the joy of Thy
faith onto the pages of my life. Amen.*

Righteousness by Faith

*And be found in him, not having mine
own righteousness . . . but . . . the righteousness which is of God by faith.*
—PHILIPPIANS 3:9

OH, IF I COULD, by God's grace, pour into
you the difference between our every day
righteousness and that attitude of a living faith
that dares claim and believe in Him! For I per-
ceive there is something after the righteousness
of faith that you can never get by the righteousness of the law.

There is something in imputed knowledge
and righteousness of God which is greater
than all beside. David speaks about it. Paul
often speaks about it. But I want to bring just
a touch of it on the lines of faith in Abraham's
life.

Abraham believed God, and it was counted
unto him for righteousness. It was an imputed
condition. God came forth and said to all the

demons in hell and all the men on the earth, "Touch not that man."

You can count on God to bring you through on all lines for "no weapon that is formed against thee shall prosper" (Isa. 54:17).

> *Lord, by faith impute Thy righteous-*
> *ness that I might stand even against*
> *the forces of hell. Amen.*

Day 12

Faith Is the Victory!

Above all, taking the shield of faith,
wherewith ye shall be able to quench all
the fiery darts of the wicked.
—EPHESIANS 6:16

REMEMBER THAT God our Father intensely
desires for us to have all the full manifestation of His power so that we need nothing but His Son. We have perfect redemption. We have all the power of righteousness. We have to understand that we are brought into line with all of God's power, dethroning the power of the enemy.

If you are afflicted in any way, do not for a moment under any circumstances come to the conclusion that the devil has enmity against you. No, he never has. The devil has nothing against you. But the devil is against the living Christ and wants to destroy Him. If you are filled with the living Christ, the devil is anxious to get you out of the way, thereby destroying Christ's power.

> *Lord Jesus, by faith I claim Your victory over the devil. Amen.*

Faith Without Charity

And though I have all faith, so that I could remove mountains, and have not charity, I am nothing.
—1 CORINTHIANS 13:2

SUPPOSE I HAD all faith so I could remove mountains; and I had a big farm, but there was some of my farm land that was not very profitable. It was stony, had many rocks upon it and some little mountains on it that were absolutely untillable and no good. But because I have faith without charity, I say, "I will use my faith, and I will move this land. I do not care where it goes so long as my land is clean." So I use my faith to clear my land.

The next day my poor neighbor next door comes and says, "I am in great trouble. All your wasteland and stony, rocky land has been tipped onto mine, and my good land is spoiled."

And I, who have faith without charity, say

to him, "You get faith and move it back!" That profits nothing.

Then when you pray, God will wonderfully answer you. Nothing will hinder your being used for God. Gifts are not only useable, but God is glorified in Jesus when you pray the prayer of faith. Jesus said, "When ye pray believing, the Father shall be glorified in the Son."

> *Heavenly Father, fill me with Thy love so that I might be used of Thee to glorify Thy name whenever I exercise faith. Amen.*

Faith Will Be Tested

Therefore being justified by faith . . . we glory in tribulations also: knowing that tribulation worketh patience; And patience, experience.

—ROMANS 5:1–4

DO YOU WANT to have a big story to tell? Well, here it is. Count it all joy in the midst of temptations. When the trial is severe, when you think that no one is tried as much as you, count it all joy. When you feel that some strange thing has so happened that you are altogether in a new order, count it all joy. When the trial is so hard you cannot sleep, count it all joy. God has something for you in the trial, something divine, something of a divine nature.

After Abraham was tried, then he could offer Isaac—not before he was tried. God put Abraham through all kinds of tests. For twenty-five years he was tested. He is called the "father of the faithful" because he would not give up when he was under trials. We have a blessing today because one man dared to believe God without moving away from Him for twenty-five years.

> *Jesus, when I am under trials, experiencing temptations, and facing tests, when I don't know what to do, I shall lean wholly on You. Amen.*

Day 15

Ask and Believe

And all things, whatsoever ye shall ask in prayer, believing, ye shall receive.
—MATTHEW 21:22

GOD WANTS US to come into the place where we will never look back. God has no room for the man who looks back, thinks back, or acts back.

The Holy Ghost wants to get you ready for stretching yourself out to Him, believing that He is a rewarder of them that diligently seek Him. You need not use vain repetition. Ask and believe.

> *Jesus, I come to Thee asking, not begging, to receive all that You have for me. Give me the patience to faithfully wait to receive what You have promised to me. Amen.*

Day 16

The Leap of Faith

Jesus saith unto her [Martha], *Said I not
unto thee, that, if thou wouldest believe,
thou shouldest see the glory of God?*
—JOHN 11:40

YOU HAVE TO take a leap today—leap into
the promises. You have to believe that
God never fails you—that it is impossible for
God to break His Word. He is from
everlasting to everlasting.

Forever and ever, not for a day
He keepeth His promise forever;
To all who believe, to all who obey,
He keepeth His promise forever.

There is no variableness with God. There is
no shadow of turning. He is the same. He
manifests His divine glory.

To Mary and Martha, Jesus said, "If thou
wouldst believe, thou shouldest see the glory
of God."

He was tempted in all points, like as we, yet without sin. He endured all things. He is our example.

> *Lord, I would take that leap of faith*
> *that I might behold Thy glory. Amen.*

Day 17

Faith Laughs at Impossibilities

Jesus said unto them . . . if ye have faith as a grain of mustard seed . . . nothing shall be impossible unto you.
                                        —MATTHEW 17:20

FOUR THINGS are emblematic, divinely ascertained or revealed by the Lord—fire, love, zeal, faith.

Fire, burning up intensely, making us full of activity on line with God.

Love, where there is nothing but pure, undefiled willingness, yieldedness, knowing no sacrifice.

Zeal, so in the will and the mighty power of God until we press beyond measure into that which pleases God.

Faith, that laughs at impossibilities, and cries, "It shall be done!"

> *Lord Jesus, set me ablaze with fire,*
> *love, zeal, and faith. Amen.*

Day 18

Believe the Atonement

*And not only so, but we also joy in God
through our Lord Jesus Christ, by whom
we have now received the atonement.*
—ROMANS 5:11

ATONEMENT is "at-one-ment." Perfect
association is being at one in Christ.
Whatever His appointment in the earth, whatever He was, we have been joined up to Him
in "one-ment."

The atonement is "one-ment," meaning
that He has absolutely taken every vestige of
human deformity, depravity, lack of
comprehension, and inactivity of faith and has
nailed it to the cross. It's forever on the cross.
You died with Him on the cross. If you will
only believe you are dead with Him, you are
dead indeed to sin and alive to righteousness.

There is not a vestige of human weakness in
His righteousness. If I dare believe, then I am
so in order with God's Son that He makes me

perfect, at one with Him, no sin, no blemish, no failure, absolutely a perfect atonement till there isn't a vestige of weakness left.

Dare you believe it? If you dare believe now, then oneness, purity, power, and eternal fact are working through you.

Lord Jesus, I believe that Thy atonement makes me one with Thee. Amen.

Day 19

Trusting an Extravagant God

Bless the Lord, O my soul: and all that is within me, bless his holy name. Bless the Lord, O my soul, and forget not all his benefits.

—PSALM 103:1–2

As I SEE IT, Scripture is extravagant. When God speaks to me, He says, "Anything you ask." When God is speaking of the world's salvation, He says, "Whosoever believes." So I have an extravagant God with extravagant language to make me an extravagant person—in wisdom.

You must learn above all things that you have to be out and God must be in you. The trouble with many people is that they never have gotten out so that He could get in. But if God ever gets in, you will be the first one out, never to come in anymore.

Jesus, by faith I go out that all of You might come in. Amen.

Have a Real Faith

*Therefore whosoever heareth these sayings
of mine, and doeth them, I will liken him
unto a wise man, which built his house
upon a rock.*

—MATTHEW 7:24

ARE YOU READY to believe the Scriptures?
The Scripture is our foundation to build
upon properly. Christ is the cornerstone. We
are all in the building.

Claim your rights in God's order. Do not
give way.

Have a real faith. Believe that love covers
you. His life flows through you. His
quickening Spirit lifts you.

*Heavenly Father, I claim the founda-
tion of Thy Word for Thy answer to
my every need. Amen.*

Day 21

Believing as a Son of God

*But as many as received him, to them
gave he power to become the sons of God,
even to them that believe on his name.*
—JOHN 1:12

BE AS A SON OF GOD. A son of God must
have power over the powers of the devil.
A son of God must behave himself
seemingly. A son of God must be temperate
in all things. A son of God must have the
expression of the Master. He should be filled
with tenderness and compassion. He should
have a body filled with bowels of mercy. A son
of God must excel in every way.

God spoke and the heavens gave place to
His voice. God proclaimed, "This is my
beloved son . . . hear ye him" (Matt. 17:5).
Afterward, Jesus always said, "I am the Son of
God."

God comes to you and says, "Behold, you
are sons of God!" Oh, that we could have a

regiment rising, claiming their rights, standing erect with a holy vision and full of inward power, saying, "I am, by the grace of God, a son of God!"

> *Lord, by Thy grace I trust in Thee and claim that I am Your son, Your daughter, Your child. Amen.*

Unwavering Faith

If any of you lack wisdom, let him ask of God . . . it shall be given him. But let him ask in faith, nothing wavering.
—JAMES 1:5–6

I AM SATISFIED that God, who is the builder of divine order, never brings confusion in His order. If you want this divine order in your life, if you want wisdom, you have to come to God believing.

God does not honor unbelief. He honors faith. For example, if you ask God once for healing, you will get it. But if you ask a thousand times a day till you forgot what you were asking, you're not asking in faith. If you would, ask God for your healing now, then begin praising Him. He never breaks His promise. You would go out perfect. "Only believe."

Lord, I set aside confusion and wavering for single-mindedness and faith. I come to You asking once in faith. I stand on Thy Word, not my vain repetitions. Amen.

Day 23

Precious Faith

. . . to them that have obtained like precious faith with us through the righteousness of God and our Saviour Jesus Christ.

—2 PETER 1:1

FAITH IN JESUS Christ gives us access to the fullness of God. It was by grace first. You were saved through grace. But now we have another grace, a grace of access; a grace of entering in; a grace of understanding the unfolding of the mystery; a grace which shall bring us into a place of the knowledge of God.

All that the Father has, all that Jesus has, all the Holy Ghost has, we have access into.

We have the right and an open door into all that God has for us. There is nothing that can keep us out. Jesus Christ is the Alpha and Omega for us, that we may know grace, favor, and mercy to lift us into and take us through.

"Grace and peace be multiplied unto you through the knowledge of God, and of Jesus our Lord" (2 Pet. 1:2). You want grace multiplied? You want peace multiplied? You have it here if you dare to believe.

We have access to the Father by faith through His grace.

> *Thank you, Father, for the grace through Jesus Christ that You have bestowed on my life. Amen.*

Day 24

Rest in Faith

For we which have believed do enter into rest.

—HEBREWS 4:3

HEN THE DIVINE has the full control, then all earthly cares and anxieties pass away. If we live in the Spirit, we are over all human nature. If we reach the climax God's Son said we had to come into, we shall always be in the place of peace.

Jesus said, "If ye abide in me, and my words abide in you, ye shall ask what ye will, and it shall be done unto you" (John 15:7). Jesus was the manifestation of power to dethrone every evil thing. He always dealt with the flesh. It was necessary for Him to say to Peter, "Get thee behind me, Satan: for thou savourest not the things that be of God, but the things that be of men" (Mark 8:33). Everything that interferes with your plan of putting to death the old man is surely the old man comforting you, so that you will not act to crucify the flesh.

It is a rest in faith, a place where you can smile in the face of any eruption. No matter what comes, you will be in the place of real rest (Matt. 11:28–29).

> *By faith, Lord, I enter into Thy rest in which there is perfect peace. Amen.*

Day 25

One Faith

There is one body, and one Spirit . . . One Lord, one faith, one baptism, One God and Father of all, who is above all, and through all, and in you all.

—EPHESIANS 4:4–5

JUST IN THE proportion that you have the Spirit unfolding to you—"One Lord, one faith, one baptism"—you have the Holy Ghost so incarnated in you, bringing into you a revelation of the Word. Nothing else can do it, for the Spirit gave the Word through Jesus. Jesus spoke by the Spirit that was in Him, being the Word. The Spirit brought out all the Word of Life. Then we must have the Spirit.

If you take up John's Gospel, you will find that when He came, it wasn't to speak about Himself but to bring forth all that the Father willed. "For all things that I have heard of my Father I have made known unto you" (John 15:15).

We shall have faith. The church will rise to

the highest position when there is no schism in the body on the lines of unbelief. When we all with one heart and one faith believe the Word as it is spoken, then signs, wonders, and various kinds of miracles will be manifested. There will be one accord, in "One Lord, one faith, one baptism." Hallelujah!

> *Lord God, by Thy Spirit we shall confess One Lord, Jesus, and be of one faith in Him. Amen.*

Holy Faith

But ye, beloved, building up yourselves on
your most holy faith, praying in the Holy
Ghost, Keep yourselves in the love of God.
—JUDE 1:20

I SAW ONE DAY a great big magnet let down amongst iron, and it picked up loads of iron and carried them away. That is a natural order, but ours is a spiritual order of a holy magnet. That which is in thee is holy. That which is in thee is pure. When the Lord of righteousness shall appear, who is our life, then that which is holy, which is His nature, which is His life, shall go, and we shall be forever with the Lord.

You have not gone yet—but you are sure to go. Seeing we are here, comforting one another, building up one another in the most holy faith, we would say, "No, Lord, let it please thee that we remain. But please, Father, let us be more holy. Let us be more pure.

Please, Father, let this life of Thy Son eat up all mortality till there is nothing left but that which is to be changed, in a moment, in the twinkling of an eye."

Ask God that every moment shall be a moment of purifying, a moment of rapture-seeking, a moment in your body of a new order of the Spirit.

Let God take you into the fullness of redemption in a wonderful way. Covet to be more holy. Covet to be more separate. Covet God. Covet holy faith.

> *Please, Father, build in me a holy faith that I might be totally set apart unto Thee. Amen.*

Day 27

Faith That Trusts

*And such trust have we through Christ to
God-ward: Not that we are sufficient of
ourselves to think any thing as of ourselves; but our sufficiency is of God.*
—2 Corinthians 3:4–5

WE WANT TO GET to a place where we are
beyond trusting ourselves. Beloved,
there is so much failure in self assurances. It is
not bad to have good things on the lines of
satisfaction, but we must never have anything
on the human plane that we rest upon.

There is only one sure place to rest upon,
and our trust is in God. In Thy name we go.
In Thee we trust. And God brings us off in
victory. When we have no confidence in ourselves to trust in our God, He has promised to
be with us at all times, to make the path
straight, and to make a way. Then we
understand how it is that David could say,
"Thy gentleness hath made me great" (2 Sam.
22:36).

Ah, thou Lover of souls! We have no confidence in the flesh. Our confidence can only stand and rely on the One who is able to come in at the midnight hour as easily as at noonday and make the night and the day alike to the man who rests completely in the will of God, knowing that "all things work together for good to them that love God," and trust Him. And such trust have we in Him. The Lord has helped me to have no confidence in myself but to trust wholly in Him, bless His name!

In Thee, Oh Lord, do I place all my trust. I will not trust in myself or in human flesh, only in Thee. Amen.

Day 28

Faith Lets Go

Let us lay aside every weight, and the sin which doth so easily beset us . . . Looking unto Jesus the author and finisher of our faith.

—HEBREWS 12:1–2

HOW MAY I get nearer to God? How may I be in the place of helplessness in my own place and dependent on God?

Let yourself go till He is on the throne. Let everything submit itself to the throne and the King.

If you will let go, God will take hold and keep you up. Oh, to seek only the will of God, to be only in the purpose of God, to seek only that God shall be glorified, not I!

Jesus, I trust You. I let go that You might be all in all. Amen.

Faith and Grace

*Therefore, it is of faith, that it might be
by grace; to the end the promise might be
sure to all the seed.*

—ROMANS 4:16

OD'S WORD SAYS, "by faith, that it may be
by grace." Grace is omnipotent, active,
benevolent, and merciful. Grace is true, perfect, and an inheritance from God that the
soul can believe.

Grace is of God. It is by faith. You open the
door by faith, and God comes in with all you
want.

Faith acts on a fact. A fact brings joy.
So you hear the Scriptures, which make
you wise unto salvation, opening your
understanding, so that if you hear the truth
and believe, you will receive what you want.
By faith you open and shut the door. By grace,
God comes in—saving, healing, and meeting
your needs.

Father, I thank You for Thy grace. By faith I open the door of my life to receive all that is in Thy grace—thy salvation, healing, and blessings in Jesus Christ. Amen.

Day 30

Living Faith

*That your faith should not stand in the
wisdom of men, but in the power of God.*
—1 CORINTHIANS 2:5

FAITH HAS the power of access. Living faith
is unfeigned faith; faith that never
wavers. Faith comes from the Author of faith.

By a living faith in God, the crooked are
made straight, the lame leap with joy, and the
blind are made free.

*Lord Jesus, birth into me Thy living
faith. Amen.*

Day 31

Praying and God's Word

He [God] *sent his word, and healed them, and delivered them from their destructions.*

—PSALM 107:20

Healing

ARE YOU READY? For what? That you may move and be moved by the mighty power of God that cannot be moved, and so chastened and built up till you are in the place where it doesn't matter where the wind blows or what difficulties arise. You are fixed on God.

Are you ready? For what? To come into the plan of the Most High God, believing what the Scripture says and holding fast to that which is good, believing no man shall take your crown.

God can so change us by His Word that we are altogether different day by day. David knew this. He said, "Thy word hath quickened me" (Ps. 119:50). "He sent his word, and healed them" (Ps. 107:20). How beautiful it is that God makes His Word abound!

If you will receive the Word of God, you will always be in a big place. If you pray about the Word of God, the devil will be behind the whole thing. Never pray about anything which is "Thus saith the Lord." It has to be yours to build you on a new foundation of truth.

> *Lord, grant me the strength and boldness to stand firm on Your Word, receiving Thy Word for all my needs. Amen.*

Day 32

Anywhere and Everywhere

Praying always with all prayer and supplication in the Spirit.
—EPHESIANS 6:18

WHEN TRAVELING by ship from England to Australia, these people came round me and said, "We want to know if you will join us in an entertainment." Then they said to me, "Well, we have a very large program and would like to put you down to sing a song."

"Oh," I said, "my song will be given just before I sing. So you cannot put it down until I am to sing."

I sang:

If I could only tell it as I know it,
My Redeemer who has done so much for me;
If I could only tell you how much He loves you,

*I am sure that you would make Him yours today.
Could I tell it? Could I tell it?*

I never could tell it. The people were
weeping all over. We had some fine young
men give themselves to Jesus.

*Father God, grant me the boldness to
transform any place I am into an
occasion for prayer. Amen.*

Believe the Word of God

*Verily, verily I say unto you, He that
believeth on me hath everlasting life. I am
that bread of life.*

—JOHN 6:47–48

TELL YOU there is a redemption, there is
an atonement in Christ, a personality of
Christ to dwell in you. There is a godlikeness
for you to attain unto, a blessed resemblance
of Christ, of "God in you" that shall not fail if
you believe the Word of God.

Were you ever able to fathom the fullness of
that redemption plan that came to you
through believing in Jesus? In the first place,
He was "of God." He was called "The Word."
He became flesh! Then, He was filled with the
Holy Ghost. Then, He became the "operation"
or "voice."

Jesus was the operation of the Word, by the
power of God through the Holy Ghost, and so
He became "the Authority."

You are born of an incorruptible power of God, born of the Word, who has the personality, the nature of God. You were begotten of God, and you are not your own. You are now incarnated, so you can believe that you have passed from death unto life and have become an heir of God and a joint heir of Christ in the measure in which you believe His Word.

Thank You, Jesus, for birthing Thy Word in me that I might live by and feed upon Thy Word continually. Amen.

The Piercing Sword

> *For the word of God is quick, and power-*
> *ful, and sharper than any twoedged sword.*
> —HEBREWS 4:12

THE WORD, the Life, the Christ which is the Word, separates in you soul from spirit—what a wonderful work! The Spirit divides you from soul affection, from human weakness, from all depravity, from the human soul in the blood of man. The blood of Jesus can cleanse your blood till the very soul of you is purified and your very nature is destroyed by the nature of the living Christ.

The greatest work God ever did on the face of the earth was done in the operation of His power. Jesus was raised from the dead by the operation of God's mighty power. The operation in our hearts of that same resurrection power will dethrone self and will build God's temple.

Callousness will have to change. Hardness will have to disappear. All evil thoughts must be gone. Raised up will be lowliness of mind. This is a wonderful plan for us. His Word transforming, resurrecting, giving thoughts of holiness, inspiring intense zeal, and giving us a desire for all of God till we live and move in the atmosphere of holiness.

> *Word of God, pierce my heart and touch my whole being with Thy resurrection power. Amen.*

Day 35

Prayer Changes Hearts

The publican, standing afar off, would not lift up so much as his eyes unto heaven, but smote upon his breast, saying, God be merciful to me a sinner.

—LUKE 18:13

I KNOW THIS as clearly as anything, that no man can change God. You cannot change Him.

But as a man labors in prayer, and groans, and travails because his tremendous sin is weighing him down, he becomes broken in the presence of God. When properly melted in the perfect harmony with the divine plan of God, then God can work in that clay where before He could not work.

Heavenly Father, change me as I pray. Amen.

You Are an Epistle

Forasmuch as ye are manifestly declared to be the epistle of Christ ministered by us, written not with ink, but with the Spirit of the living God.

—2 Corinthians 3:3

IT IS TRUE that we must be the epistle of Christ. The epistle of Christ is a living power in the mortal flesh, quickening, dividing asunder everything which is not of the Spirit, till you realize that now you live in a new order. It is the Spirit that has manifested Himself in your mortal body, the Word has become life.

For you to live is to be His epistle, emblematic, divinely sustained by another power greater than you. So you do not seek your own anymore. You are living in a place where God is on the throne. He reigns in your human life. God is changing you and making you understand this wonderful truth—you are Christ's epistle!

Christ, make of my life Thy epistle to the world. Write Thy salvation, Thy holiness, Thy redemption, Thy good news on my heart that others may read in me only of Thee. Amen.

Day 37

Bethel

And Jacob awaked out of his sleep, and he said, Surely the Lord is in this place; and I knew it not. . . . And he called the name of that place Bethel.

—GENESIS 28:16, 19

IS HE YOUR God? He is the God of the sinner. Oh, there is something wonderful about it. He is the God of the helpless. He is full of mercy. I tell you He is your God, and He is prepared to meet you exactly as He met Jacob.

Jacob had deceived in every way. He had deceived to get his birthright; to get his cattle. He was a deceiver. Truly, the devil had a big play with Jacob, but, praise God, there was one thing that Jacob knew. Jacob knew that God fulfilled His promises.

There in Bethel, God let Jacob see the ladder, and it was a wonderful ladder, for it reached from earth to heaven. He saw angels ascending and descending. I am glad that the angels began at the bottom and came to the top. It was a lovely ladder, I tell you, if they could begin at the bottom and go to the top.

Just like Jacob in prayer, we begin at the bottom and go to the top.

Bethel—the place of prayer; the place of changing conditions; the place where we start on earth and enter heaven.

> *Father, I come to Bethel, Thy house of prayer, to start on earth and to climb into the heavenlies, for I long to be with Thee. Amen.*

Day 38

The Word in Your Heart

Thy word have I hidden in mine heart,
that I might not sin against thee.
—PSALM 119:11

IWOULD LIKE the day to come that we would never come to a meeting without having the Word of God with us. The great need today is more of the Word. There is no foundation apart from the Word.

The Word not only gives you foundation, but it puts you in a place where you can stand, and after the battle keep on standing. Nothing else will do that.

When the Word is in your heart, it will preserve you from the desire to sin. The Word is the living presence of that divine power that overcomes the world. You need the Word of God in your hearts that you might be able to overcome the world.

*Lord, I will meditate on Thy Word
Prepare my heart that I might hide
Thy Word therein and be so strength-
ened that I may have no desire of sin
in me. Amen.*

Day 39

Believe the Word of God

And they overcame him [the devil] by the blood of the Lamb, and by the word of their testimony; and they loved not their lives unto the death.

—REVELATION 12:11

HAVE WE BEEN with Jesus? Do not think you will comfort people by singing wonderful hymns—they are lovely. Do not think you will comfort people any other way but by the Word of God being manifest because you have been with Jesus. There must be the law of the Spirit of life in Christ Jesus that shall put to death every other thing but His Word.

It is one thing to read the Word of God. It is another thing to believe it.

It is possible to be real and earnest and have zeal and fastings, and yet not to have faith. Do you not know that one little bit of faith which can only come through the Word of God is worth more than all your cryings, all your rolling on the floor, and all your screaming?

God is better than all of this.

May the Holy Ghost give us today an inward knowledge of what it is to believe the Word of God. It is God's purpose to make every believer able to subdue everything and to be whole, perfect, and an overcomer in Christ.

> *Word of God, richly indwell me that I might have an overcoming faith to subdue all worldly things in my life. Amen.*

Day 40

Praying in Prison

Giving no offence in anything, that the ministry be not blamed; But in all things approving ourselves as the ministers of God . . . in imprisonments.

—2 CORINTHIANS 6:3–5

IN SWITZERLAND I have been put in prison twice for this wonderful work. But, praise God, I was brought out all right!

The officers said to me, "We find no fault. We are so pleased. We have found no fault because you are such a great blessing to us in Switzerland." And in the middle of the night they said, "You can go."

I said, "No, I will only go on one condition. That is that every officer there is in this place gets down on his knees and I pray with all of you." Glory to God!

Lord, in the midst of my prisons, give me the wisdom to pray and not to moan and groan. Amen.

Day 41

The Word and the Kingdom

Let the word of Christ dwell in you richly in all wisdom; teaching and admonishing one another . . . singing with grace in your hearts to the Lord.

—COLOSSIANS 3:16

I BELIEVE THAT God wants to bring to our eyes and our ears a living realization of what the Word of God is, what the Lord God means, and what we may expect if we believe it. I am certain that the Lord wishes to put before us a living fact which shall by faith bring into action a principle which is within our own hearts, so that Christ can dethrone every power of Satan.

Come, this is my point. The kingdom of heaven is within us, within every believer. The kingdom of heaven is the Christ, is the Word of God.

The kingdom of heaven is to outstrip everything else, even your own lives. It has to be so manifested that you have to realize even the death of Christ brings forth the life of Christ.

The kingdom of heaven is the life of Jesus; it is the power of the Highest. The kingdom of heaven is pure; it is holy. It has no disease, no imperfection.

> *Word of God, stir up richly within me that the kingdom of heaven might be manifested. Amen.*

Day 42

Praying as the Spirit Prays

But the Spirit itself maketh intercession for us with groanings which cannot be uttered.

—ROMANS 8:26

WE MUST HAVE life in everything. Who knows how to pray but as the Spirit prayeth? What kind of prayer does the Spirit pray? The Spirit always brings to your remembrance the mind of the Scriptures and brings forth all your cry and your need better than your words. The Spirit always takes the Word of God and brings your heart, and mind, and soul, and cry, and need into the presence of God.

So we are able to pray only as the Spirit prays, and the Spirit only prays according to the will of God, and the will of God is all in the Word of God. No man is able to speak according to the mind of God and bring forth the deep things of God out of his own mind.

Now I can see that the Holy Ghost so graciously, so extravagantly puts everything to one side that He may ravish our hearts with a great inward cry after Jesus.

> *Holy Spirit, ravish my heart. Set aside all distractions. Pray through me that my heart's cry might be heard in the presence of God. Amen.*

The Word, Not Feelings

When ye received the word of God . . . ye received it . . . as it is in truth, the word of God, which effectually worketh also in you that believe.

—1 THESSALONIANS 2:13

OH, THAT GOD shall give us an earnest, intent position where flesh and blood have to yield! We will go forward. We will not be moved by our feelings.

The man is prayed for tonight and gets a blessing, but tomorrow, because he does not feel exactly as he thinks he ought to feel, begins murmuring. So, he exchanges the Word of God for his feelings.

Let Christ have His perfect work. You must cease to be. That is a difficult thing for you and me. But it is not trouble at all when you are in the hands of the Potter. You are only wrong when you are kicking. You are all right when you are still and He is forming you afresh.

So let Him form you afresh today and make

of you a vessel that will stand the stress.

> *Word of God, take priority over my feelings that I must trust only Thy truth. Amen.*

Day 44

God's Truth in Our Hearts

But the word is very nigh unto thee, in thy mouth, and in thy heart, that thou mayest do it.

—Deuteronomy 30:14

I BELIEVE THAT God wants to bring our eyes and our ears to a living realization of what the Word of God is, what the Lord God means, and what we may expect if we believe it.

I am certain that the Lord wishes to put before us a living fact which shall, by faith, bring into action a principle which is within our own hearts, so that Christ can dethrone every power of Satan.

It is only the truth of God's Word revealed to our hearts that can make us so much greater than any idea of ourselves that we had.

I believe that there are volumes of truth right in the midst of our own hearts. There is the need for revelations and for stirring

ourselves up to understand the mightiness
which God has within us. We may prove what
He has accomplished in us if we will only be
willing to accomplish that which He has
accomplished in us.

> *Lord, reveal Thy Word in my heart*
> *that I might know Thy mighty power*
> *in my life. Amen.*

Day 45

Loving God's Word

How sweet are thy words unto my taste
yea, sweeter than honey to my mouth.
—PSALM 119:103

ONE THING God has given to me from my youth up is a taste or relish for no other book except the Bible. I can say before God, I have never read a book but the Bible, so I know nothing about books.

As I have peeped into books, I have seen in some of them perhaps one reason for good people to say, "That is a good book." Oh, but how much better to get the Book of books which contains nothing but God. If a book is commended because it has something about God in it, how much more shall the Word of God be food for the soul, the strengthening of the believer, and the building up of the human order of character with God, so that all the time he is being changed by the Spirit of the

Lord from one state of glory into another.

We shall become flat, anemic, and helpless without the Word, dormant and so helpless to take hold of the things of God.

The Word is everything. The Word has to become everything. When the heavens and the earth are melted away, then we shall be as bright, brighter than the day, and going on to be consistent because of the Word of God.

> *I love Thy Word, Oh God. It is sweet to my taste and life to my being. Thy Word I cherish with my whole heart. Amen.*

The Word Imparts Life

It is the spirit that quickeneth; the flesh profiteth nothing: the words that speak unto you, they are spirit, and they are life.
—JOHN 6:63

ONE THING that the saints need to get to know is not how to quote Scripture but how the Scripture should be pressed out by the Spirit that the Spirit should impart life as the Word is given. Jesus says, "My word is the spirit of life."

There is a lovely word along this line in the eleventh chapter of 1 Corinthians: "For if we would judge ourselves, we should not be judged. But when we are judged, we are chastened of the Lord, that we should not be condemned with the world" (vv. 31–32).

Word of God, press in on my heart that the Spirit might press it out of me in Jesus' name. May I not simply quote Scripture to those I meet everyday, but may I rather impart the life of Christ to those who need Him. Amen.

Day 47

Sanctified by Thy Word

*Sanctify them through thy truth: thy
word is truth.*

—JOHN 17:17

THY WORD is truth. Sanctify them
through Thy Word, which is truth. No
child of God ever asks a question about the
Word of God. What do I mean? The Word of
God is clear on breaking bread, on water baptism, and on so many things. No person who
is going on to obedience and sanctification of
the Spirit will pray over the Word. The Word
of God is to be swallowed, to be obeyed, not
to pray over.

If you ever pray over the Word of God,
there is some disobedience. You are not willing
to obey. If you come into obedience of the
Word of God, then when it says anything
about water baptism, you will obey. When the
Word speaks about tongues you will obey

what it says about speaking in tongues. When the Word says anything about breaking bread and assembling yourselves together, you will obey.

When you are sanctified by the Spirit, you will be obedient to everything revealed in God's Word. In the measure you are not obedient, you will not come into the sanctification of the Spirit.

Holy Spirit, sanctify me by Thy truth and Word, that I might obey Thy Word without reservation. Amen.

Day 48

Take the Word of God

As for God, his way is perfect: the word of the Lord is tried: he is a buckler to all those that trust in Him.

—PSALM 18:30

SO I PRAY that you will think seriously in your heart about this: You have to be in the world, but not of it. Be a personal manifestation of the living Christ. Just as Christ was walking about the earth, you have to walk about as a son of God, with power and manifestation, because the people have not time to read the Bible, so you have to be the walking epistle, "read and known of all men."

You have to see rightly that Jesus is the Word. You have to believe the Word of God, not change it because people have other opinions.

In taking God's Word, you will discover that you want nothing better because there *is* nothing better. It is in His Word that you will find all you want—food when you hunger; light in your darkness; largeness of heart; and thoughts inspired by God.

> *Lord, Thy Word will stand no matter what man says. Thy Word satisfies my every need. It is sustenance for my spirit; it guides my feet aright and inspires my mind to godliness. Amen.*

Day 49

Prospering in the Word

*This book of the law shall not depart out
of thy mouth . . . for then thou shalt make
thy way prosperous, and then thou shalt
have good success*

—JOSHUA 1:8

GOD WANTS strong people. Remember the charge God gave Joshua when he said, "Be strong and of a good courage . . . neither be thou dismayed" (Josh. 1:9). And then He gave him the charge. If God forecasts anything for you, He will give you the power to carry it through.

So, after He had given Joshua the Word, He said, "Now it will depend upon your living, day and night, meditating on the Word of God."

"Then thou shalt have good success." He told Joshua that, in this state of grace, whenever he put his foot down, not to let it slide back, but to put the other foot ready for going forward.

There are some things for certain. First, you

will never forget your sins. Second, God has forgotten them. Third, the devil will try to make you remember your sins. The question is, are we going to believe God, the devil, or ourselves? God says our sins are passed, cleansed, gone! You cannot go on with God till you stand on His Word as "cleansed," with the heart made pure.

Jesus, I believe Thy Word, not mine or the devil's. I am cleansed from all my sin by Thy blood. Hallelujah! Amen.

Day 50

The Word in You

*I am crucified with Christ: nevertheless I
live; yet not I, but Christ liveth in me.*
—GALATIANS 2:20

THE SONS of God are being manifested.
Glory is now being seen. The Word of
God is becoming so expressed in the life of a
son of God that natural life is ceasing and the
Word begins to live fully in him.

How can Christ live in you? There is no way
for Christ to live in you but only by the manifested Word in you, through you, manifestly
declaring every day that you are a living epistle
of the Word of God.

Beloved, God would have us to see that no
man is perfected or equipped on any lines
except as the living Word abides in him.

It is the living Christ; it is the divine likeness of God; it is the express image of Him;
and the Word is the only factor that works out

in you and brings forth these glories of identification between you and Christ. It is the Word dwelling in your hearts, richly by faith.

> *Word of God, indwell me so richly that others might see Thee in me. Amen.*

Day 51

The Living Word in You

*In the beginning was the Word, and the
Word was with God, and the Word was
God. The same was in the beginning with
God.*

—JOHN 1:1–2

ALL WAS MADE by the Word. I am begotten
by His Word. Within me there is a substance that has almighty power in it if I dare
believe. Faith going on to be an act, a reality, a
deposit of God, an almighty flame moving you
to act, so that signs and wonders are manifest.
A living faith within an earthen casket.

Are you begotten? Is it an act within you.
Some need a touch, a liberty to captives. As
many as He touched were made perfectly
whole. Faith takes you to the place where God
reigns, imbibing God's bountiful store.
Unbelief is sin, for Jesus went to death to bring
us the light of life.

God in you is a living substance, a spiritual
nature, the living Word. You live by another

life, the faith of the Son of God.

As the Holy Ghost reveals Jesus, He is real, the living Word, effective, acting, speaking, thinking, praying, singing in you.

> *Word of God, birth in me the life of Jesus Christ that He might live fully in me. Amen.*

Day 52

Prayer and Faith

Therefore I say unto you, What things soever ye desire, when ye pray, believe that ye receive them, and ye shall have them.
—MARK 11:24

WHILE I KNOW prayer is wonderful, and not only changes things, but changes you, while I know the man of prayer can go right in and take the blessing from God, yet I tell you that if we grasp this truth that we have before us, we shall find that faith is the greatest inheritance of all.

May God give us faith that will bring this glorious inheritance to our hearts. Beloved, it is true that the just shall live by faith; and do not forget that it takes a just man to live by faith. May the Lord reveal to us the fullness of this truth that God gave to Abraham.

He wants to bring us into that blessed place of faith, changing us into a real substance of faith, till we are so like-minded with Him that whatever we ask, we believe; and believing, we receive; and our joy becomes full because we believe.

> *As I pray, Lord, fill me with faith, so that by believing Your Word, I might ask and receive. Amen.*

The Foundation

Therefore whosoever heareth these sayings of mine, and doeth them, I will liken him unto a wise man, which built his house upon a rock.

—MATTHEW 7:24

IF WE ARE EVER going to make any progress in divine life, we shall have to have a real foundation. There is no foundation, only the foundation of faith for us. All our movements, and all that ever will come to us, which is of any importance, will be because we have a rock. If you are on the Rock, no power can move you. The need of today is the Rock to have our faith firm upon.

Your faith must have something to establish itself on.

If you build on anything else but the Word of God—on imaginations, on sentimentality, or any feelings, or any special joy—it will mean nothing to you without a foundation on the Word of God.

Upon the solid rock of Your Word, I build my life, Jesus. You are my Rock; You are my foundation. Amen.

Day 54

Founded Upon a Rock

When the flood arose, the stream beat vehemently upon that house, and could not shake it: for it was founded upon a rock.

—LUKE 6:48

I WAS GOING on a tram from London to Blackpool. A man who was a builder stood next to me, and I asked him, "Are men building those houses upon the sands?"

"Oh, you don't know? You're not a builder," he said. "Don't you know that we can pound that sand till it becomes like rock?"

"Nonsense," I said. I saw an argument was not going to profit, so I dropped it. By and by we reached Blackpool where the mountainous waves come over the shore. I saw a row of houses that had fallen flat, and drawing the attention of this builder, I said, "Oh, look at those houses. See how flat they are." He forgot our previous conversation, saying, "You know, here we have very large tides. Those houses built on the sands, when the tides came in, fell flat."

Beloved, it won't do to build on sand.

Jesus, Your Word is the foundation for all things. Amen.

Day 55

Praying in Harmony

They were all filled with the Holy Ghost . . . and the multitude of them that believed were of one heart and of one soul.

—ACTS 4:31–32

GOD LIFTS the church in prayer into a place of manifested reconciliation, oneness of accord, until the devil has no power.

Whatsoever things ye desire when ye pray, only believe! How the Master can move among the needs and perishing when He has the right of way in the church!

Let us be in harmony, in one accord, as we pray with the divine plan having knowledge connected with love.

Lord, teach us to pray together in such unity and in one accord that by faith we might see You do great and mighty things in the church. Amen.

Day 56

Incorruptible Seed

Being born again, not of corruptible seed,
but of incorruptible, by the word of God,
which liveth and abideth for ever.
—1 PETER 1:23

YOU ARE BORN of an incorruptible power—the power of God's Word—by His personality and His nature. Ye are begotten of God and are not your own. You are now incarnated. You can believe that you have passed from death unto life and become an heir of God, a joint heir with Christ, in the measure that you believe His Word.

The natural flesh has been changed for a new order. The first order was the natural Adamic order. The last order is Christ—the heavenly order. And now you become changed by a heavenly power existing in an earthly body; a power that can never die. It can never see corruption, and it cannot be lost.

I want you to see that you are born of a

power which exists in you, a power of which God took and made the world that you are in.

> *Thank You, Lord, that I have the privilege to be born of Thy incorruptible seed, Thy Word. Amen.*

Day 57

Victory in the Word

But thanks be to God, which giveth us the
victory through our Lord Jesus Christ.
—1 CORINTHIANS 15:57

THERE IS a power in God's Word which
brings life where death is. To him that
believeth this Word, all things are possible.

The Life of the Son is in the Word. Jesus
brought life and immortality to our lives
through the gospel.

There is a river, the streams of which make
glad the city of God. Jesus Himself has con-
quered death and given us the victory!

Jesus, Thou art the Word of God that
giveth us the victory over sin and
death. Amen.

Day 58

The Supernatural Word

All scripture is given by inspiration of God, and is profitable for doctrine, for reproof, for correction, for instruction in righteousness.

—2 TIMOTHY 3:16

ALL OUR HOPE is in the Word of God. The Word of God abideth forever. Never compare the Book of books with other books. It is from heaven. It doesn't contain the Word of God. It *is* the Word of God. Supernatural in origin; eternal in duration and value; unequaled in scope; and divine in authorship is God's Word.

You cannot have the knowledge of the Word without joy. Have eternal faith—daring to believe what God has said!

Thank You, Father, for the written Word that reveals Your plan of salvation in Christ Jesus. Amen.

Day 59

The Profit of the Word

For unto us was the gospel preached, as well as unto them: but the word preached did not profit them, not being mixed with faith in them that heard it.

—HEBREWS 4:2

THE WORD quickens the preacher, the hearer and everybody. The Word giveth life, and God wants it to be so alive in you that you will be moved as it is preached. Oh, it is lovely to think that God can change you in a moment and can heal you in a moment. When God begins, who can hinder?

Sometimes a thing comes before me, and I realize that nothing but the Word of God can do it. I meet all classes of people—people who have no faith—and I find the Word of God quickens them, even those who have no knowledge of salvation. The Gospel of the Lord Jesus Christ *does* cure everything.

My dear ones, it is impossible for God to fail you. If you hear the Word of God, it will stimulate you to know as sure as you live that God will bring you out of this condition.

Oh, Word of God, quicken me, stimulate me, heal me, save me in Jesus' mighty name. Amen.

Day 60

The Spirit Prays in Us

We know not what we should pray . . . but the Spirit itself maketh intercession for us.
—ROMANS 8:26

HOW DO YOU come to God? Where is God? Is He in the air? In the wind? He that cometh to God, where is He? God is in you. Oh, hallelujah! And you will find the Spirit of the Living God in you, which is the prayer circle; which is the lifting power; which is the revelation element; which is the divine power that lifts you.

He that cometh to God is already in the place where the Holy Ghost takes the prayers and swings them out according to the mind of the Spirit. For who hath known the mind of Christ, or who is able to make intercession but the mind of the Spirit of the Living God. Where is He? He is in us!

God answers prayers because the Holy

Ghost prays; your advocate is Jesus; and the Father is the judge of all. There He is. Is it possible for any prayer to miss on those lines?

> *Spirit of God, pray in me, through me, and in spite of me. Amen.*

Day 61

Far Better to Go

For to me to live is Christ, and to die is gain.

—Philippians 1:21

BELIEVE that it is possible for God to sweep a company right into the glory before the rapture just as well as at the rapture. May God grant unto us a very keen inward discerning of our heart's purity. We want to go. It is far better for us to go, but it is far better for the church that we stay.

If you could but comprehend this word of truth that Paul spoke, "It is far better for me to go," you would never take a pill or use a plaster. You would never do anything to save yourself from going if you believed it was better to go. There is a definite, inward motion of the power of God for the human life to so change that we would not lift a finger, believing it was far better to go.

"Lord, for the purpose of being a blessing, further for Thy sake and for the sake of the church, just keep us full of life to stay."

Jesus, going on with You is better than life itself. I desire to be filled with Thy life now and forever. Amen.

Day 62

Gifts of Healing

*For to one is given by the Spirit . . . the
gifts of healing by the same Spirit.*
—1 CORINTHIANS 12:8–9

HOLY GHOST people have a ministry. I
pray that all the people which have
received the Holy Ghost might be so filled
with the Holy Ghost that, without having
the gift, the Holy Ghost within them brings
forth healing power.

That is the reason why I love to have people
help me when I am praying for the sick. There
are people who have a very dim conception of
what they possess in God's Spirit.

I deal with the gift, not gifts, of healing.
There is a difference. Gifts of healing can deal
with every case of sickness, every disease that
there is. It is so full, beyond human expression,
but you come into the fullness of it as the light
of God's healing reveals it to you.

The divine gift of healing is so profound in a person with it that there is no doubt and could not be. Whatever happens would not change the man's opinion, thought, or act. He expects the very thing that God intends him to have as he lays hands on the seeker.

Holy Spirit, use Your gift of healing in me. Amen.

Day 63

Healed by His Word

He sent his word, and healed them, and delivered them from their destructions.
—PSALM 107:20

YOU CAN BE healed if you will hear the Word. This Word says it is by faith, that it might be by grace. Grace is omnipotence. It is activity, benevolence, and mercy. It is truth, perfection, and God's inheritance in the soul that can believe.

Grace is God. You open the door by faith, and God comes in with all you want. It cannot be otherwise, for it is, "of faith that it might be by grace" (Rom. 4:16).

This is believing, and most people want healing by feeling. It cannot be.

By Thy Word, not my feelings, I am healed. Hallelujah!

His Spirit in Us

*But the manifestation of the Spirit is
given to every man to profit withal.*
—1 CORINTHIANS 12:7

GOD HAS privileged us in Christ Jesus to
live above the ordinary human plane of
life. Those who want to be "ordinary" and live
on a lower plane, can do so; but as for me, I
will not!

We have the same God that Abraham
and Elijah had. We need not come behind
in any gift or grace. We may not possess
the abiding gifts, but if we are full of the
Holy Ghost and divine unction, it is possible,
when there is need, for God to manifest every
gift of the Spirit through us to give a
manifestation of the gifts as God may choose
to use us.

This ordinary man Stephen became mighty
under the Holy Ghost's anointing. He stands

supreme in many ways among the apostles.

"And Stephen, full of faith and power, did great wonders and miracles among the people" (Acts 6:8). Stephen was just as ordinary as you and me, but he was in the place where God could so move upon him that he, in turn, could move all before him. He began in a most humble place and ended in a blaze of glory. Beloved, dare to believe in Christ!

> *Holy Spirit, empower me to go beyond the ordinary to the extraordinary through Thy power and unction. Amen.*

Day 65

Healing Without Hands

And as many as touched him [Jesus] *were made whole.*

—MARK 6:56

WHEN THE presence of the Lord is there to heal, it does not require hands. Faith is the great operation position. When we believe God, all things are easy. When I went to Sweden, they would not let me lay hands on people for healing.

So they built places where I could speak to thousands of people in Sweden.

To all the people I said, "All of you that would like the power of God going through you today, healing everything, put your hands up." Thousands of hands went up.

I prayed. "Lord, show me how it can be done today without the people having hands laid upon them." And He told me as clearly as anything to pick a person out that stood upon a rock. To her I said, "Tell all the people your troubles." She began to relate her troubles from her head to her feet. She was in so much pain.

"Lift your hands high," I said. "In the name of Jesus, I rebuke the evil one from your head to your feet. I believe He has loosed you."

Oh, how she danced and jumped and shouted! Hundreds were healed without a touch and hundreds saved with touching. Our God is a God of mighty power.

> *Lord, I need no touch but Thine to heal me. Amen.*

Day 66

Salvation and Healing

When Jesus saw their faith, he said unto the sick of the palsy . . . I say unto thee, Arise, and take up thy bed, and go thy way into thine house.

—MARK 2:5, 10–11

BEFORE LEAVING home, I received a wire telling me that I should go to Liverpool. There was a woman with cancer and gall stones who was down with much discouragement. If I know God is sending me, my faith rises. God sent me to her.

The woman said, "I have no hope."

"Well," I said, "I have not come from Bradford to go back home with a bad report."

God said to me, "Establish her in the fact of the new birth." When she had the assurance that her sin was gone and she was born again, she said, "That [salvation] is everything to me. Cancer is nothing now. I have Jesus!"

The battle was won. God delivered her. She was free from sin and disease. She got up,

dressed, and was happy in Jesus.
Will you believe?

> *Jesus, You are my salvation and my*
> *healing. I believe that You alone can*
> *set me free from sin and sickness.*
> *Amen.*

Day 67

Filled With the Spirit

*And be not drunk with wine, wherein is
excess; but be filled with the Spirit.*
—EPHESIANS 5:18

THERE IS a necessity for every one of us to
be filled with God. It is not sufficient to
have just a "touch," or to be filled with a
"desire." The only thing that will meet the
needs of the people is for you to be immersed
in God so that whether you eat or drink, or
whatever you do, it may be all for the glory of
God. In that place you will find that all your
strength, mind, and soul is filled with a zeal,
not only for worship, but for proclamation.

That proclamation will be accompanied by
all the power of God, which must move
Satanic power, disturb the world, and make it
feel upset.

The reason the world is not seeing Jesus is
because Christian people are not filled with

Jesus. They are satisfied with weekly meetings, occasionally reading the Bible, and sometimes praying. Beloved, if God lays hold of you by the Spirit, you will find that there is an end of everything and a beginning of God so that your whole body becomes seasoned with a divine likeness of God.

> *Fill me, Holy Spirit. May those people with whom I come into contact daily see only Jesus when they look at my life. Make me a divine likeness of God. Amen.*

God's Resurrection Touch

*Then Peter said, Silver and gold have I
none; but such as I have give I thee: In the
name of Jesus Christ of Nazareth rise up
and walk.*

—ACTS 3:6

A MAN WHO had spent years in a wheelchair
but who had been healed, came on the
platform and told how he was loosed. Another
person with a blood issue for many years testified. A blind man told how he got his eyes
opened.

I said to the people, "Are you ready?" Oh,
they were so ready. A dear man got hold of a
boy who was encased in iron from top to
bottom, lifted him up and placed him on the
platform. Hands were laid upon him in the
name of Jesus.

"Papa! Papa! Papa!" he said. "It's all over me!
O Papa, come take these irons off!" And the
father took the irons off. Healing had gone all
over the boy.

This is what I feel. The life of God is going all over me, the power of God is all over me.

Let it go over us, Lord, the power of the Holy Ghost, the resurrection of heaven, the sweetness of His benediction, and the joy of the Lord!

Touch me, Lord, with Thy resurrection power, Thy blessing, and Thy joy. Amen.

Day 69

Casting Out Devils

For he [Jesus] said unto him, Come out of the man, thou unclean spirit.

—MARK 5:8

AFTER MANY calls, letters, and requests, I went to London. When I got there, the dear father and mother of the needy one took my hands, led me up onto a balcony, and pointed to a door that was open a little. I went in that door and have never seen a sight like it in my life.

I saw a young woman, beautiful to look at, but she had four big men holding her down to the floor. Her eyes rolled, and she could not speak. She was exactly like that man who saw Jesus and ran out from the tombs.

The power of Satan was so great upon this beautiful girl that she whirled and broke away from the four strong men.

The Spirit of the Lord was wonderful in me,

and I went right up to her, looked into her face, seeing the evil powers there.

Her very eyes flashed with demon power. "In the name of Jesus," I said, "I command you to leave! Though you are many, I command you to leave this moment in the name of Jesus."

She instantly became sick and vomited out thirty-seven evil spirits, giving them a name as they came out. That day she was made as perfect as anybody.

> *At the name of Jesus, every demon must flee. Amen.*

Day 70

It Is Finished

When Jesus therefore had received the vinegar, he said, It is finished: and he bowed his head, and gave up the ghost.
—JOHN 19:30

WHEN I WAS in Cazadero seven or eight years ago, amongst the first people that came to me in those meetings was a man who was stone deaf. Every time we had a meeting, as I rose to speak this man would take his chair from the ordinary row and place it right in front of me. The devil used to say, "Now you're done."

I said, "No, I am not done. It is finished." After the meeting had been going on for three weeks, one night as we were singing this man became tremendously disturbed. He looked in every direction. He became as one that had almost lost his mind.

Then he took a leap. He started on the run and went out amongst the people. He went out about sixty yards away and heard singing. The Lord said, "Thy ears are open."

The man came back, and we were still singing. That stopped our singing. He told us that when his ears were opened, there was such a tremendous noise, he could not understand what it was. He thought something had happened to the world. He ran out of the meeting. As he got outside, he heard the singing.

> *Lord, by faith we claim Your completed, miraculous work in our lives. It is finished! Amen.*

Day 71

Hindering Evil Spirits

Beloved, believe not every spirit, but try the spirits whether they are of God: because many false prophets are gone out into the world.

—1 John 4:1

ONE DAY I met a friend of mine in the street and I said, "Fred, where are you going?"

"I am going . . . Oh, I don't feel I ought to tell you," he said. "It is a secret between God and me."

"Now we have prayed together. We have had nights of communication. We have been living in the Spirit," I said. "Surely there is no secret that could be hid from me by you."

"I'm going to a spiritualistic meeting," he said.

"Don't you think that's dangerous?" I asked.

"No," he said. "They are having some special mediums from London." He meant to say they were having some people from London more filled with the devil than we had in

Bradford. They were special devils.

"I am going," he said, "with the clear knowledge that I am under the blood."

"Tell me the results," I requested. He agreed.

Later he told me that the seance had begun, the lights went low, and everything was dismal.

The mediums had tried every possible thing they could for over an hour to get under control. Then the light went up and they said, "We can do nothing tonight. Some here believe in the blood."

A million thanks, Lord, for the blood of Jesus. Cover me, my family, and all around me with the powerful blood of Jesus. Amen.

Day 72

Our Chief Executive

But the Comforter, which is the Holy Ghost, whom the Father will send in my name, he shall teach you all things.
—JOHN 14:26

A CHIEF EXECUTIVE is one who has a right to declare everything on the board. The chief executive in the world is the Holy Ghost. He is here today as a communicant to our hearts, to our minds, to our thoughts, saying whatever God wants us to know.

So this Holy Executive in us can speak wonderful words. The Spirit will teach you, bring all things to your remembrance. You need not have any man teach you, but the unction abideth and you need no teachers.

This is the office of the Holy Spirit. This is the power of His communication. This is what Paul means when he says, "God is love." Jesus, who is grace, is with you. But the Holy Ghost is the speaker. He speaks everything concerning Jesus.

Holy Spirit, speak to me. Teach me that I may know, understand, and apply the Word. Amen.

Fullness of the Spirit

> *For John truly baptized with water; but*
> *ye shall be baptized with the Holy Ghost*
> *not many days hence.*
>
> —ACTS 1:5

THERE ARE three things in life, and I notice that many people are satisfied with only one. There is blessing in justification; in sanctification; and in the baptism of the Holy Spirit.

Salvation is a wonderful thing, and we know it. Sanctification is a process that takes you on to a higher height with God. Salvation, sanctification, and the fullness of the Spirit are processes

Any number of people are satisfied with "good"—that is justification or salvation. Other people are satisfied with "better"—that is a sanctified life, purified by God. Other people are satisfied with the "best"—that is the fulless of God with revelation from on high.

So I come to you with the fullness of God in the Holy Spirit through His baptism. I come not with good, but better; not with better, but with best.

> *Heavenly Father, I thank Thee for the goodness of Thy salvation, the going on with Thee through sanctification and the baptism of Thy Spirit. Amen.*

Day 74

Sanctified by the Spirit

Elect according to the foreknowledge of God the Father, through sanctification of the Spirit, unto obedience and sprinkling of the blood of Jesus Christ.

—1 Peter 1:2

THERE IS a sanctifying of the human spirit. It does not matter what you say, if your human spirit does not get wholly sanctified, you will always be in danger. It is that position where the devil has a chance to work on you.

Therefore, we are taught to come into sanctification, where the rudiments, the uncleanness, the inordinate affections and corruptions pass away because of incorruption abiding. In sanctification, all kinds of lusts have lost their power.

This is the plan. Only in the ideal pursuit of this does God so bless us in our purifying state that we lose our earthly position and ascend with Him in glory. The saints of God, as they go on into perfection and holiness, understanding the mind of the Spirit and the law of the Spirit of life, are brought into a very blessed place—the place of holiness, the place of entire sanctification, the place where God is enthroned in the heart.

The sanctified mind is so concentrated in the power of God that the saint thinks about the things that are pure and lives in holy ascendancy, where every day he experiences the power and liberty of God.

Sanctify me, Holy Spirit, that I may be filled with Thee, not me. Amen.

Day 75

Healed by His Stripes

But he was wounded for our transgressions, he was bruised for our iniquities: the chastisement of our peace was upon him; and with his stripes we are healed.
—Isaiah 53:5

WENT TO visit a sick woman whose address was given to me in Belfast. At her house, a young man met me at the door and pointed me to go up the stairway. When I got up onto the landing, there was a door wide open, so I walked right into the doorway and found a woman sitting up on the bed. As soon as I looked at her, I knew she couldn't speak to me, so I began to pray.

She was moving backward and forward, gasping for breath. When I prayed the Lord said to me, "Read Isaiah 53." When I got to the fifth verse, the woman shouted, "I am healed!"

"Oh," I said, "Woman, tell me."

She said, "Three weeks ago I was cleaning

the house. I moved some furniture, strained my heart and moved it out of its place. The doctors examined me and said I would die of suffocation. But last night, in the middle of the night, I saw you come into my room. When you saw me you knew I couldn't speak, so you began to pray. Then you opened to Isaiah 53 and read until you came to the fifth verse. When you read the fifth verse, I was completely healed. That was a vision. Now it is a fact."

I know that the Word of God is true!

Jesus, by Your stripes I am healed. Amen.

Day 76

The Holy Spirit Quickens

But if the Spirit of him that raised up Jesus from the dead dwell in you, he . . . shall also quicken your mortal bodies by his Spirit that dwelleth in you.
—ROMANS 8:11

MANY PEOPLE are receiving a clear knowledge of an inward working power from the Spirit which is not only quickening their mortal bodies, but also pressing into that natural body an incorruptible power which is manifesting itself, getting ready for the rapture.

It is the inward life, the new man in the old man, the new nature in the old nature, the resurrection power in the dead form, the quickening of all, the divine order of God manifested in the human body that quickens us, giving us life. The nature of the living Christ gives us power over all death.

Do not be afraid to claim the quickening, life-giving power of the Holy Spirit. That is power over all sin, power over all disease.

The former law was of the natural man. Now the new law is of the life of the Spirit or the manifestation of the new creation, which is Christ in us, the manifested power of the Glory. Glory is a manifestation of a divine nature in the human body.

Holy Spirit, quicken my body with Thy divine nature and glory. Amen.

Day 77

Why Wait on the Holy Spirit?

But wait for the promise of the Father . . . For John truly baptized with water; but ye shall be baptized with the Holy Ghost not many days hence.

—ACTS 1:4–5

THE DISCIPLES tarried at Jerusalem till they were endued with power from on high. We know that the Holy Ghost came. It was right for them to tarry. It is wrong now to wait for the Holy Ghost to come. He has come!

Then why are we waiting? Why do we not all receive the Holy Ghost? Because our bodies are not ready for it. Our temples are not cleansed. When our temples are purified and our minds put in order, then the Holy Ghost can take full charge. The Holy Ghost is not a manifestation of carnality.

The Holy Ghost is most lovely. He is the great refiner. He is full of divine, not natural life. Don't wait. I desire for you to lift your minds, elevate your thoughts, come out of the world into a place where you know that you have rest for your feet.

Desire the inrushing river of the Holy Ghost—a pure, holy, and divine river of living water to flow through you. Not later. Now!

> *Holy Spirit, purify my heart, my life.*
> *Flow in me and through me, now.*
> *Amen.*

Day 78

Divine Healing

Bless the Lord, O my soul, and forget not all his benefits: Who forgiveth all thine iniquities; Who healeth all thy diseases.
—PSALM 103:2–3

THE GIFT of divine healing is more than audacity, more than unction. People sometimes come to me very troubled. They will say, "I had the gift of healing once, but something has happened, and I do not have it now."

You never had it. "Gifts and calling of God are without repentance" (Rom. 11:29). If you fall from grace and use a gift wrongly, it will work against you. If you use tongues out of the will of God, interpretation will condemn you. If you have been used and the gift has been exercised and you have fallen from your high place, it will work against you.

It seems almost then as though you have never been born. The jealousy God has over us, the interest He has in us, the purpose He has for us, the grandeur of His glory are so marvelous. God has called us into this place to receive gifts.

> *Lord, thank You for the wonderful sense of life that has been given to me through Your Holy Spirit. I seek to be used by Your Holy Spirit that I might use Your gifts for Your glory. Amen.*

The Spirit in You

And I [Jesus] *will pray the Father, and he
shall give you another Comforter, that he
may abide with you for ever.*

—JOHN 14:16

THERE IS a difference between the Spirit
being in you and the Spirit being with
you. For instance, we are getting light now
from outside this building. This is exactly the
position of every believer that is not baptized
with the Holy Ghost. The Spirit is with every
person that is not baptized, and they have light
from the outside. But suppose all the light that
is coming through the window was inside.

That is exactly what is to be taking place.
We have revelation from outside, revelation in
many ways by the Spirit, but after He comes
inside, it is revelation from inside which will
make things outside right.

We are baptizing people in water, remem-
bering that they are put to death, because

every believer ought to be covered. Every believer must be put to death in water baptism.

The baptism of the Spirit is to be planted deeper until there is not a part of you that is left. There is a manifestation of the power of the new creation by the Holy Spirit right in our mortal bodies.

Where once we were, now He reigns supreme, manifesting the very Christ inside of us, the Holy Ghost fulfilling all things right there.

> *Spirit of God, go with me and immerse me with Thy living water that You might reign in all of me. Amen.*

Day 80

Faith and Healing

But Jesus turned him about, and when he saw her, he said, Daughter, be of good comfort; thy faith hath made thee whole.
—MATTHEW 9:22

MORE AND MORE I see that day in which the Lord's visitation is upon us so that the presence of the Lord is here to heal. We should have people healed in meetings in which I speak while they are under the unction of the Holy Spirit.

I have been preaching faith so that you may definitely claim your healing. I believe if you listen to the Word and are moved to believe, and if you stand up while I pray, you will find healing virtue loosed in you.

When you were saved, you were saved the moment you believed. You will be healed the moment you believe.

Lord, I desire a touch from You that will shake the foundation of all my weakness. Grant me the faith to receive the healing You have for me in Jesus' mighty name. Amen.

Day 81

Wind, Person, and Fire

He that believeth on me, as the scripture hath said, out of his belly shall flow rivers of living water.

—JOHN 7:38

JESUS SPOKE about the Holy Ghost which was to be given. In Acts 2 we find three manifestations of the Holy Ghost—wind, person, and fire. The first manifestation is a rushing mighty wind. Second, there are cloven tongues of fire. Think of the mighty wind and the cloven tongues of fire over everyone. Third, see the incoming and outflowing of the Holy Ghost.

Can we be filled with this river? How is it possible for us to flow as a river?

You will never get to know God better by testimony. Testimony should always come through the Word. You will not get to know God better by prayer. Prayer has to come out of the Word. The Word is the only thing that reveals God and is going to be helpful in the world. When the breath and the presence of God come, the Holy Spirit speaks expressively according to the mind of the Father and the Son.

When you are filled with the person of the Holy Ghost, then the breath, the power, the unction, the fire of the Spirit takes hold of the Word of Life, which is Christ. God wants to fill you with that divine power so that out of you will flow living waters.

> *May the fire, wind, and person of the Holy Spirit fill me, that out of me will flow living waters that others might know Jesus through me. Amen.*

God Doesn't Bring Disease

God . . . cause his face to shine upon us . . . That thy way may be known upon earth, thy saving health among all nations.

—PSALM 67:1–2

SOME PEOPLE talk about God being pleased to put disease on His children. "Here is a person I love," says God. "I will break his arm. In order that he should love me more, I will break his leg. In order that he should love me still more, I will give him a weak heart. And in order to increase that love, I will make him so that he cannot eat anything without having indigestion."

The whole thing won't stand daylight. Is it right now to say, "You know, my brother, I have suffered so much in this affliction that it has made me know God better"? Well, now, before you get up, ask God for a lot more affliction, so you will get to know Him better still. If you won't ask for more affliction to make you purer still, I won't believe that the first affliction made you purer; because if it had, you would have more faith in it. It appears you haven't faith in your afflictions. Language doesn't count unless it works out a fact. But if the people can see that your language is working out a fact, then they have some grounds for believing in it.

I have looked through my Bible, and I cannot find where God brings disease and sickness.

It isn't God at all, but the devil that brings sickness and disease.

> *In Jesus' name, I rebuke disease and sickness. Lord God, You are the Great Physician. I declare healing in Your mighty name. Amen.*

Walk and Live in the Spirit

That the righteousness of the law might be fulfilled in us, who walk not after the flesh, but after the Spirit.

—ROMANS 8:4

WE MUST know that the baptism of the Spirit immerses us into an intensity of zeal, into a likeness to Jesus, to make us into pure, running metal, so hot for God that it travels like oil from vessel to vessel.

This divine line of the Spirit will let us see where we have ceased and He has begun. We are at the end for a beginning. We are down and out, and God is in and out.

There isn't a natural thought of any use here. There isn't a thing that is carnal, earthly, natural, that can ever live in a meeting.

No man is able to walk spiritually without being in the Spirit. He must live in the Spirit.

He must realize all the time that he is growing in the same ideal of his Master, in season and out of season, always beholding the face of the Master, Jesus.

> *Holy Spirit, immerse me that Thy zeal will run hot in my life for Jesus Christ. May I never stop growing more and more Christlike through Your power. Amen.*

Day 84

The Spirit Reveals the Son

And hope maketh not ashamed; because the love of God is shed abroad in our hearts by the Holy Ghost which is given unto us.

—ROMANS 5:5

THE LOVE of God is shed abroad in our hearts by the Holy Ghost. The manifestation of the revelation of God's Son by the Holy Ghost comes by the Holy Spirit who is revealing Him to us as so uniquely divine that He is in power of overcoming, in power of purity, in power of rising all the time.

The Holy Ghost is shed abroad in our hearts for the very purpose that we may know that the inner man in us has to go on to develop—it must not cease growing. The Holy Ghost in us creates development and empowers us to move out as the Lord would have us be.

You are being changed, made right, made ready, changed by regenerating.

The Lord's life is moving and flowing. Put your spirit into the joy of the breath of God. Let yourself go on the bosom of His love. Be transformed by all the Spirit's life from above.

Holy Spirit, grow the image of Christ in me that I might reveal His love in my life. Change me and make me ready to be Your servant through the transformation of Your presence in my life. Amen.

Day 85

The Life of the Spirit

*And Joshua . . . and Caleb . . . spake unto
all the company of the children of Israel,
saying . . . fear them not.*
—Numbers 14:6, 9

THE SPIRIT was so mighty upon Joshua
and Caleb that they had no fear. The
Holy Spirit upon them had such a dignity of
reverence to God that these two people
brought the bunches of grapes and presented
them to the people. There were ten people sent
out. They had not the Holy Spirit and came
back murmuring.

I am speaking about people who get the
Holy Ghost and go on with God, not about
the people who remain stationery.

I pray that the same Holy Spirit on Joshua
and Caleb will fill you and search your hearts.
Be filled with the life of the Spirit that we call
unction, revelation and force. What do I call
force? Force is that position in the power of

the Spirit where, instead of wavering, you go through. Instead of judgment, you receive truth.

> *Holy Spirit, fill me with Thy boldness*
> *and power to go on with Thee and not*
> *to waver or murmur. Amen.*

Full of Faith

And the saying pleased the whole multi-tude: and they chose Stephen, a man full of faith and of the Holy Ghost.

—ACTS 6:5

SOMETHING happened in the life of this man [Stephen], chosen for menial service, and he became mighty for God.

As I read about Stephen in Acts 6 and 7, I have a vision of this scene in every detail— the howling mob with their vengeful, murderous spirits ready to devour this holy man; and he, "being full of the Holy Ghost," gazing steadfastly into heaven. From his place of helplessness, he looked up and said, "Behold, I see the heavens opened, and the Son of man standing at the right hand of God."

Is that the position that Jesus went to take?

No!

He went to sit at the right hand of the Father; but in behalf of the "first martyr," in behalf of the man with that burning flame of Holy Ghost power, God's Son stood up in honorary testimony of him who, called to serve tables, was faithful unto death.

This man chosen for an ordinary task but filled with the Holy Ghost was so moved upon by God that he finished his earthly work in a blaze of glory, magnifying God with his last breath. Friends, it is worth all to gain that spirit. What a divine ending to the life and testimony of a man that was "chosen to serve tables."

> *Lord Jesus, fill me with faith and the Holy Spirit, that I might blaze with Thy glory like Stephen, no matter what I face in life. Amen.*

Day 87

Our Inheritance

In whom [Christ] also we have obtained an inheritance . . . That we should be to the praise of his glory, who first trusted in Christ.

—EPHESIANS 1:11–13

GOD SAYS you are not of this world; you have been delivered from the corruption of the world; you are being transformed by the renewing of your mind. God says that you are a royal priesthood, a holy people, belonging to the building and Christ is the great cornerstone.

The Holy Spirit is coming forth to help you claim your inheritance. Do not be afraid of getting rich or of coming in, but be very afraid if you do not come in. Have God's mind on this. God says you have to overcome the world; you must have this incorruptible, undefiled position now within the human body, transforming your mind, even your very nature.

The glorious incarnation of the Spirit is your inheritance. This is where God wants to make you His own in such a way that you will deny yourself, the flesh, and the world. You can reign in this life by this lovely place, this inheritance in Christ Jesus sealed by the Holy Spirit.

Holy Spirit, seal me in Thy inheritance of glory through the precious name of Jesus. Amen.

Intoxicated by the Spirit

*And be not drunk with wine, wherein is
excess; but be filled with the Spirit.*
—EPHESIANS 5:18

WHEN YOU ARE intoxicated with the
Spirit, the Spirit life flows through the
avenues of your mind and the deep perception
of the heart with deep throbbings.

You are so filled with the passion of the
grace of God, that you are illumined by the
power of new wine—the wine of the kingdom,
the Holy Ghost—till your whole body is
intoxicated.

This is rapture! There is no natural body
that can stand the process of this going forth.
It will have to leave the body at His coming.
But the body will be a preserver to it until the
sons of God are marvelously manifested.

This holy new life, this preservative of the
Son of God in your human body, this life in

you is so after the order of God that it is not ashamed in any way to say you are coming into co-equality with the Father, with the Son, and with the Holy Spirit.

> *Thank You for allowing my life to be filled with the preservative of Your Son's presence within my human body. Fill and intoxicate me, O Holy Spirit, that I might live and move in Thee. Amen.*

Day 89

Is Healing the Main Thing?

But seek ye first the kingdom of God, and his righteousness; and all these things shall be added unto you.

—Matthew 6:33

JESUS CAME to make us free from sin—free from disease and pain. When I see a person diseased and in pain, I have great compassion for them, and when I lay my hands upon them, I know God means for men to be so filled with Him that the power of sin shall have no effect upon them. They shall go forth, as I am doing, to help the needy, sick, and afflicted.

But what is the main thing? To preach the kingdom of God and His righteousness.

Jesus came to do this. John came preaching repentance. The disciples began by preaching repentance toward God and faith in the Lord Jesus Christ.

I tell you, beloved, if you have really been

changed by God, there is a repentance in your heart never to be repented of.

Through the revelation of the Word of God, we find that divine healing is solely for the glory of God, and salvation is to make you to know you now have to be inhabited by another, even God, and you have to walk with God in newness of life.

> *Jesus, Thou art the One who not only saves the body, but Thou hast saved my soul and spirit. Wholeness is found only in Thee. Amen.*

Day 90

Unity in the Spirit

Endeavoring to keep the unity of the Spirit in the bond of peace.

—EPHESIANS 4:3

BELOVED, I want you to remember that the church is one body. She has many members, but we are all members of that one body. At any cost, we must keep the body in perfect unity.

As the church is bound together in one Spirit, the people of the church have one voice, one desire, and one plan. When the church has the mind of the Spirit with Christ, nothing can then break the church.

Holy Spirit, make me a force and power for Thy unity within the body of Christ. Amen.